Call them Canadians

Produced by
the National Film Board of Canada

Executive Producer Lorraine Monk

The Photographers

Dunkin Bancroft	Edith Karkutt	John Reeves
Jean-Paul Bernier	Guenter Karkutt	Henri Rossier
Hans Blohm	Yousuf Karsh	Jean Roy
Douglas Boult	Michel Lambeth	Michael Semak
Bob Brooks	Joan Latchford	William Staley
Jean Bruneau	André Le Coz	Lionel Stevenson
Marcel Cognac	David Leigh	Sam Tata
John de Visser	Chris Lund	Irene Taylor
Lutz Dille	Bruno Massenet	Jeremy Taylor
Vittorio Fiorucci	John Max	Evelyn Vance
Tibor Gatszegi	Jean-Paul Morisset	Werner Vollmann
Pierre Gaudard	Dik Nye	Jeanne White
Ted Grant	Gustave Pellerin	Doug Wilkinson
Richard Harrington	Sophia Pryce	Betty Williamson
George Hunter	Nina Raginsky	

Poems by Miriam Waddington

Here are the Canadians . . . young and old, anxious
and serene, the lonely and the loved ones. Here,
for the first time in the history of our country is
an intimate photographic look at the people of
Canada. The book deliberately refrains from
identifying people by their geographic locale or
ethnic origin for this is not a socio-economic study
or a statistical review of Canadians. There is not
even a record of where the photograph was taken.
It does not matter. The photographic moment
alone is supreme.

This is not a formal picture album, with best
profile to the camera. The pictures present a
candid look at Canadians, going their indi-
vidual ways in the daily pursuit of their own
private worlds. Here is the work of 44 photogra-
phers who succeeded in capturing some significant
or unforgettable moment in the lives of the people
who passed before their cameras. The poems by
Miriam Waddington, which were especially
written for this book, have been arranged to set
the mood or theme for the series of pictures which
are grouped about them. No direct reference or
relationship is intended between the actual persons
in the pictures and the thoughts conveyed in the
poetry. The poems were not written as caption
material, but only to reveal, in another artistic
medium, some further aspect of the human story.

L.M.

Call them Canadians

A photographic point of view
Produced by the National Film Board of Canada

Editor   Lorraine Monk

Poems   Miriam Waddington

Designer   Leslie Smart

Extracts from the following works
by Miriam Waddington are reprinted by
permission of the publishers:

'*Lovers*'
'*Three Poems for my Teacher*' and
'*Journey to the Clinic*'
from 'The Second Silence'
RYERSON PRESS, Toronto, 1955

'*Committee Work*' and
'*The Oracle*'
from 'The Glass Trumpet'
OXFORD UNIVERSITY PRESS, Toronto, 1966

Published by ROGER DUHAMEL FRSC Queen's Printer / Ottawa / Canada

Printed in Canada / 1968   Catalogue Number S.P. 72-2

What is a Canadian
anyway? A mountain, a maple
leaf, a prairie, a Niagara fall,
a trail beside the Atlantic, a
bilingualism, a scarred mosaic,
a yes-no somehow- or-other maybe
might-be should-be could-be
glacial shield, grain elevator,
empire daughter imperial order of
man woman child or what?

Through the dark trumpets
of north and south
through the iron gates
of east and west
the music blows loud
clanging   hangs taut
restrained   elegant
as an animal   and

regular as moons
the city tides advance   are
trapped in sewers   traffic signs
are blind   the streets are
bare   the sound is turned off:
where are all the people?

I'd like a little farm
with a house that's painted blue
with a lively little terrier
and a pussy cat or two.

I'd build a little barn
to keep my gentle cows
outside I'd build a pig-pen
for piglets and for sows;

I'd plant a little orchard
with apple and with plum
and all the birds would praise
their green kingdom.

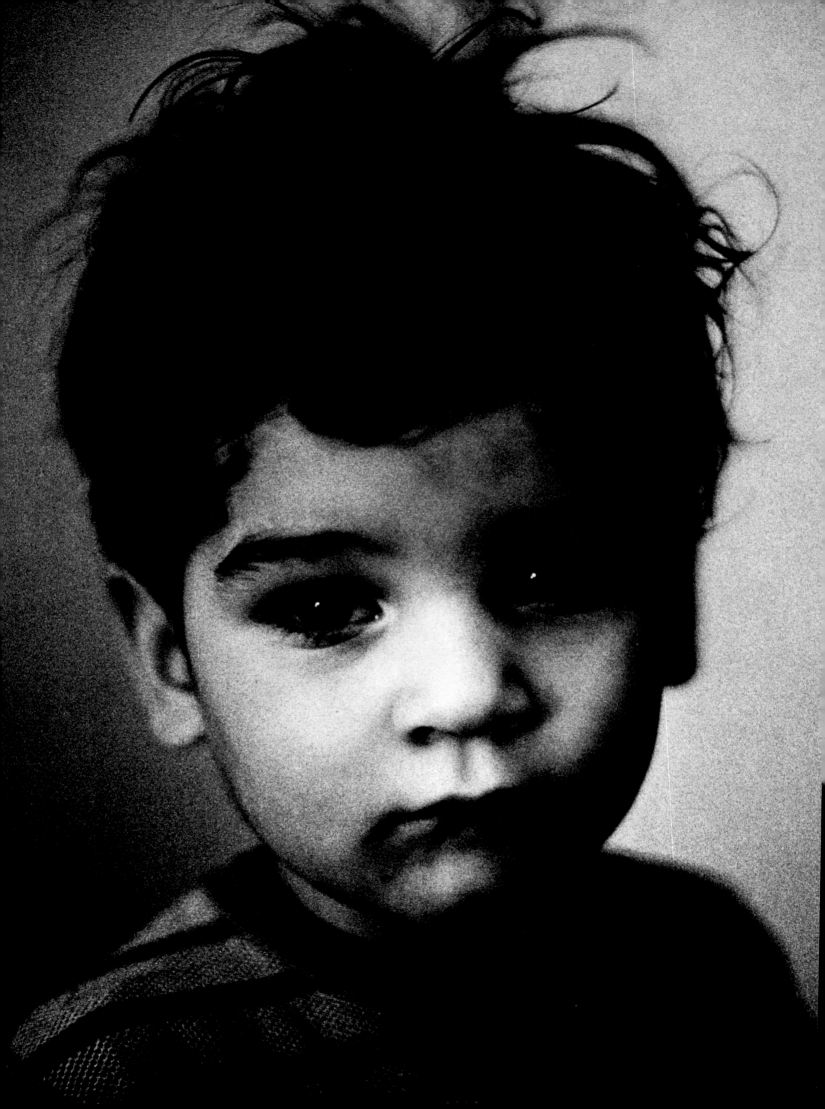

Dark is the winter water:
dead swans make it foul,
he aches and forever reaches
for the distant moving water
but a wintry man can't know
what it means to be
touched and entered
by spring's new elements
and the icy man can't know
how it feels to be caught
swift centre
in that bright undertow

I have to hurry:
                    but before I go
I want to give you
the very first words
                    of summer
and invent
            especially and only
                        for you
a completely new language
                    giddy
as butterflies
            burning
as prairie sunsets
But I have to hurry or
my words are not my words:
                    at dawn
I fall into a
            dumbness
my words close:
            at noon
they scatter
and the newsboy gathers them
                        public
in at every corner
and calls them
                promiscuous
out to every comer

It was oranges in California
the dream I mean all gold circles
that early morning in Winnipeg
with the sun crowding rays together

Into a gold volley pushing and pelting
me out of sleep—wake up, wake up!
*But my oranges, mother, they're growing
on trees and I have to pick them!*

Now? It was not God-appointed:
so I had to leave them growing there
in my dream, sunstained spaincastled
snowfresh and I wonder where

They are growing now in whose dream;
and what child in which northern city
wakes now to the cold morning
to wonder who is staying behind

Still in the dream to pick the oranges
from the children's everlasting tree?

Does your mind
curve back to Jordan river
where the road ends and the blind
Pacific unrolls naked in sunshine?
Are your dreams
swift underwater travellers
on the ocean floor
entwined anemones and
coral branching high?

What of a smile that leaps
like a white waterfall
turning joyous cartwheels
in the sun?
And tell me if you
are colored with the green notion
of dark-spaced orchards
clustering on the ridge
just above Shuswap
where the lake begins?

Little children, fishes in the net
of doctors and their instruments
you are the captives here;
locked inside a sleep
of counted minutes you will wake
to morning filled with fluttering cries
missing a tooth or curiously
gazing at bandaged arm or thigh:
is this the place, the station of your dream?

from 'The Second Silence'
RYERSON PRESS, Toronto, 1955

When I step out and feel the green world
its concave walls must cup my summer coming
and curving hold me
beyond all geography in a transparent place
where water images cling to the inside sphere
move and distend as rainbows in a mirror
cast out of focus.

And this crystal chrysalis
shapes to green rhythms to long ocean flowings
rolls towards the sun with sure and spinning speed,
and under the intensely golden point
warms expands
until walls crack suddenly
uncup me into large and windy space.

Time makes him old
but full of hope he falls
to age more slowly   unaware
that time has left him
and will not support
his thriving offshoots,
will bastardize his
darling moments   send hours
to wait in institutes
his sleep in hostels
and on his eager plate
will ladle the just dole

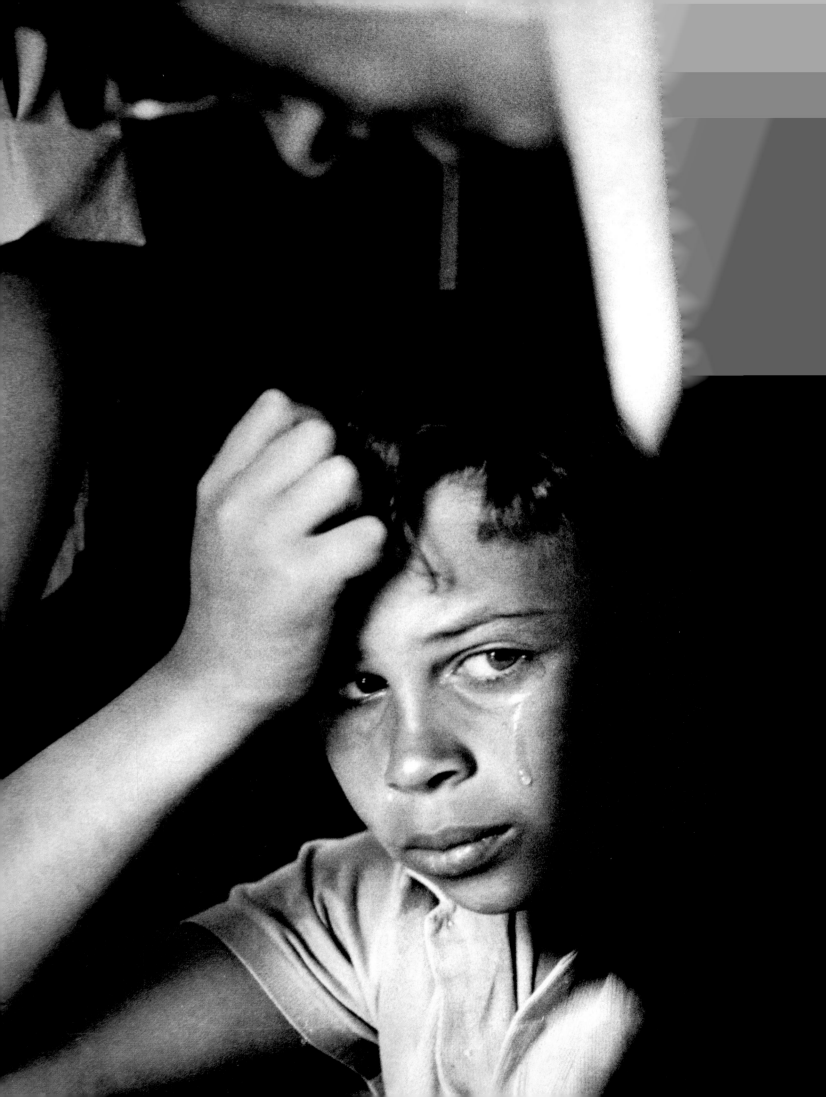

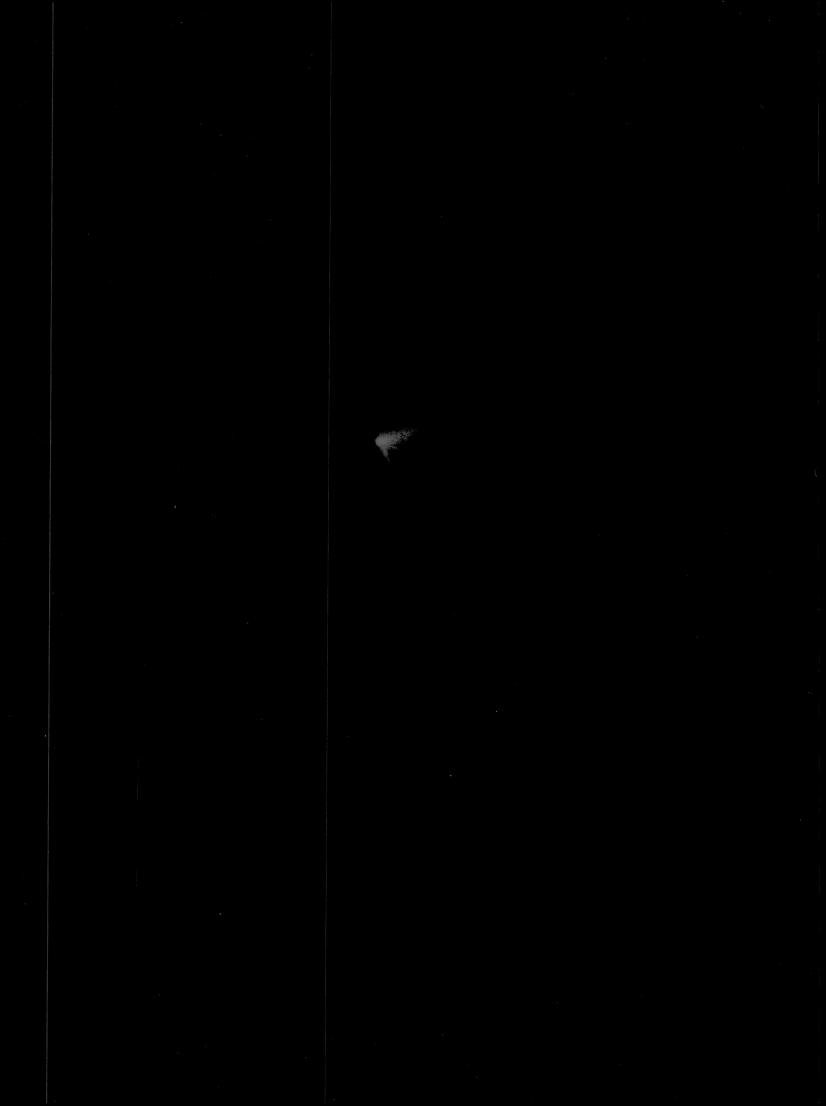

The meadow was awash with brown
and the slippery glaze of rain
after four days falling
had coated the fields with wetness;
the gulls like a paper chase hovered
over the scooped-out pools   hung
over the hollows.

Only the small boys knew
where the foxes lay hidden,
how narrow and warm they waited
close in their darkness
coveting the unfolding white
of gulls' wings   their strong stretch
elbowing distance and pushing the sky
beyond caves   brown burrows
and burials.

We are light
as dandelion
parachutes we
land anywhere
take the shape
of wherever we
fall

We are often
the size of
grasshoppers in
a jungle of grass
or we're squirmy
chains of willow
catkins

then we become
curly seashells
knobby little
swimmers in
a sea of air

lying on our backs
our eyes fly up
higher than kites
airplanes   clouds
winds   higher
than stars

we stare down
at the little
distant world
and we laugh
laugh laugh

And the mind fills
with imagined love
portioned space
and February's first
cool daffodils

From the country of the snow
spring comes upon us with a lifted brow
with *how so* and *who*
and watch her flowery lip
her almond eyes
exclaim amused surprise

Professor Waddington will not be
joining the academic procession
she wrote a note to the Dean she
said that her gown was moth-eaten
and she had to stay home to tie up
the chrysanthemums or else they
would flop all over and kill the grass
and she would have to resod around
the flowerbeds a nuisance so she regrets
she will not be able to join the academic
procession if you ask me that woman has
a nerve she's not friendly and further-
more I hear that she keeps late hours
looks at men what kind of example is that
for young girls all I can say is some
people are never satisfied

Friends when they meet
                    give greetings,
When they part
                    leave gifts;
I have left gifts
                    all over the world
and taken words
                    books smiles
kept
        even the stares of strangers
                                    in subways:
and in foreign countries
                        I have left the gift
of hope that all children
                        may walk and breathe
and laugh
            anywhere in the world
as freely
        as surrounded by friends
as in their own countries.

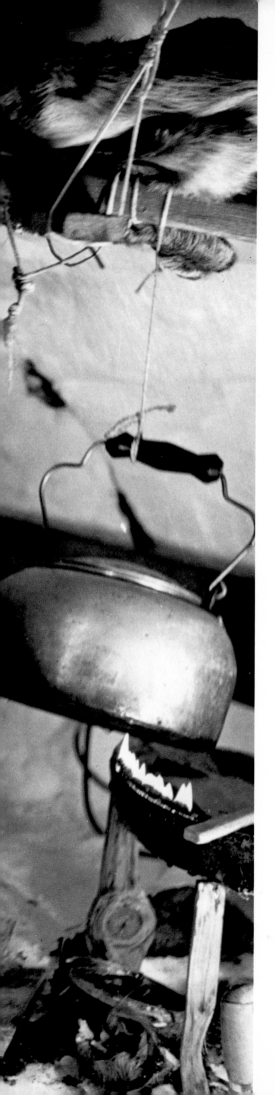

we are not one but two
we are not two but four
we are not four but many
sometimes
    we
       are
          not
             any.

We'll turn the animals
into a noah's ark
and to our new land
take spotted leghorns
mica mines black swans
and daisies of michaelmas
to bloom on garbage dumps.

I am in exile
therefore I dream
of new kingdoms
fabled as oz and
fantastic as smoke-stacks
thrusting themselves
in a chorus of color
from river to sky

we become
        the enchanted
land of ourselves
      we leap
over rainbows and
             fly
across winds we
           are bewitched
by the jasmine of faces
        by the
oleander of sound

Hey, what's this?
Sand-colored riffled clay, pure
lake pleasure, and such a bland blind
enterprise of sky (mercifully
without intelligence),
come on, baby orchards, hurry;
get up from the ploughed and flooded fields,
keep out of those puddles
or your feet will get wet
and your bark will be scalded;
don't you know this is pneumonia weather?

Stop time
          sit
               stare
unlock the last silent world
of the galleries where hang
my secret deaths

Crazy man crazy and
ruffled as roosters
we believe in brotherhood
yeah yeah

lord byron and us —
mamma-boys or cushy
teddy-toys   or maybe
little fauntleroys

our creed is the
open collar   yeah
yeah   the girls
have had the ruffles
to themselves
too long   time
for a change

we're hard   sharp
new   stamped by the die
of the man-making —
machine   yeah   crazy
and like we said:
there is a pleasure
in the pathless
woods

go cook up a storm

Rootless slumber stemless lies
broken on the coverlet
jungle dreams and butterflies
grow upon my island bed;

they overrun the ocean floor
while tigers from the cupboards walk
and agony leaps through the door
against a wall of feathered rock.

Love was a young leap across
the arc of night that separates
our planets   a milkwhite
starpricked horse clearing
horizon's hurdle wonderful
country of the future
green and white and
undulating

quiet as the world after midnight
quiet quiet is my thought of you

I wait till all the people are asleep
so my thought can touch you you   only you

let this be my poem to you
you you you   only you

Spring-rain falls
on the opening leaves
                of chestnut trees
wets
        the shabby pavements
                            makes them
dark   glistening
                breathless.

A girl with red stockings
                    short sleeves
and a proud forward-pointing nose
carries a black umbrella;
                    a plumed waterbird
she cruises
            the sea of streets.

A boy in a collegeblue
                    windbreaker
with two stripes on his sleeve
                    is promoted
ambassador of April   he carries
an armful of flowers
                    in a crumpled field
of green paper   and

Farther on a man
                    in a claycolored uniform
and peaked cap pulls
a rack
        of freshly-cleaned clothes
from his truck   and hangs them
over his arm
            a billowing harvest.

The spring-rain falls
                on the lawns   pavements
stop-signs   pleasure palaces
passers-by
            on everybody
but the rain does not quicken
a consoling thought
                grow a kind word
or nourish
            in me the hope for hope

In me spring-rain
                    awakens
only pictures
                of the times
when I sat
            with your arms around me
on a shabby sofa
                    in a room smelling of mildew,
and through the open window
                            under the curtains
came the persistent sound
                        the fresh smell
of spring-rain;

We could hear the wind
                    outside
composing poems
                    on the windowpane
with the rain
            keeping time
a metronome,
            but we could not know
how fate
        was composing the future
for us and we could not tell

How the pictures would fade,
but I can still see
                the shabby sofa,
and in that room
                your arms are still
around me your touch
                is still upon me
gentle
        dark breathless
as spring-rain

Winter folds a velvet ear
and summer's silk of corn
reflects in autumn's russet eye
the skeleton of a thorn.

An ancient map of checkered brown
engraved in multi-copper modes
unfolds against the hazy fields
four separate attitudes:

the singing eye the greening frond
join their soundings to compose
a season's score of elegies
for the monolithic rose:

and east the ellened ocean flows
while summer widows in the south
and winter holds his breath of snow
in autumn's poker mouth.

I have built a temple
in the stone body of
a man   I have
touched the seed in
the beautiful body
of a man

six angels will I set to watch
the seed of your sleep
and I will drop pain sweet as honey
over the bare tongue
and feather my stitches
soft as thighs and tender
will be my care
tender as all your years
gentle as girl grief

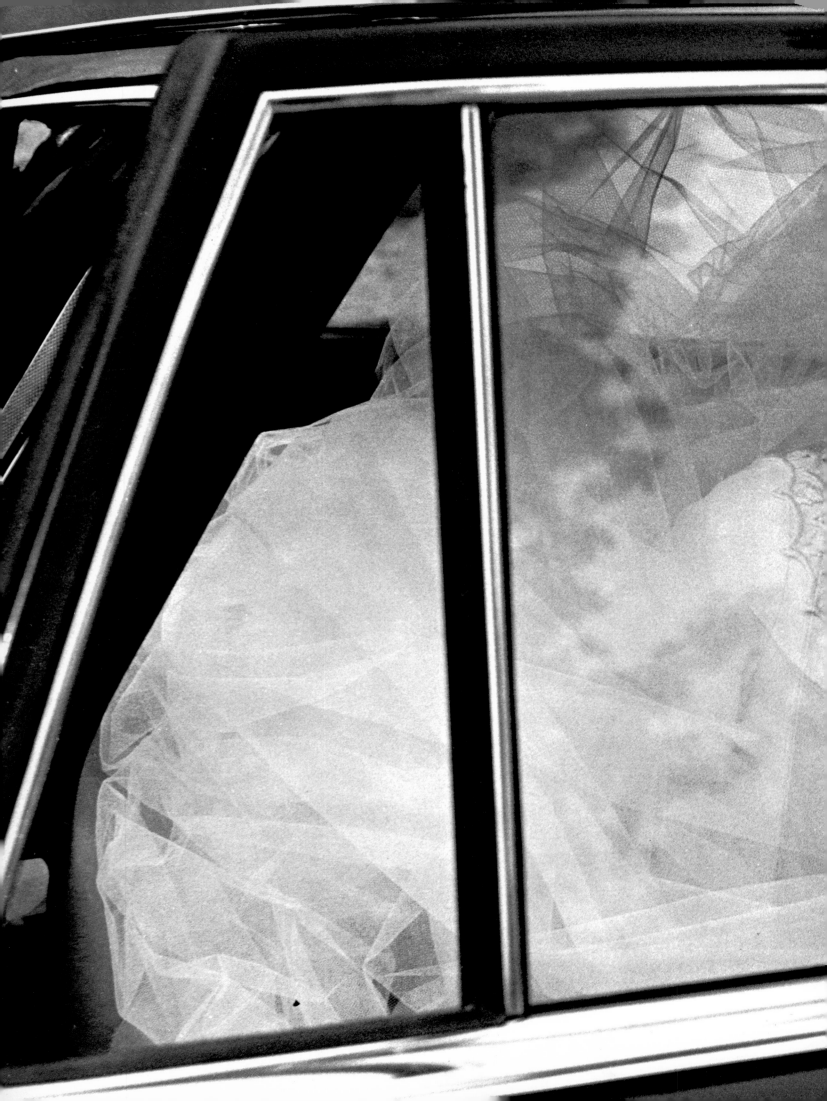

it is all city driving
past empty factories at night
with the forty mile speed limit
or the thirty-five:
                    (and for ramp speed
slow down to twenty
                    stay in your own lane
squeeze left   yield   ) it is all
in the shifting of gears the
finely meshed adjustment

(but on the parkways
                    anything goes)

Stiff as flowers
lined up beside park benches
the child hockey-players
parade their colors;
under the heavy helmets
their eyes weave a garland
of constant wonder.

Who has planted them
in the forest of winter
so far from their childhood?
Who are those giant spectators
who chopped down the summer
and now fill the arena
with loud expectation?

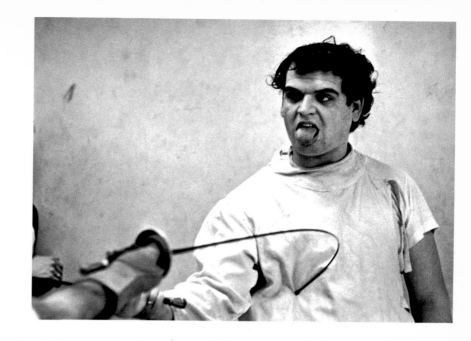

Adult education
        I think about it
driving home for lunch
           preoccupied I see
the department of highways men
          in blazing helmets
burning the brush beside the road
         and further on
the red and blue houses
          of don mills shining
in the bare and merciless light
           while joseph-colored
hudson bay blankets
          are airing on clotheslines

and still further on
           the kindergarten children
weightless
          as scattered leaves
blown here and there on the streets
          are homeward bound holding
their drawings in front of them
           like colored flags.

Proud creators   workmen
          who burn brush
mothers
          who air blankets
           children
who make pictures dance
          the sun is spilling you
in helter-skelter procession
          all over my thoughts
and setting up tents
          for a carnival
           a whole country
a huge canvas
          a riotous celebration
of a new school
          order   airiness   joy

125

I live this long winter
watch the snow whorls
and dream the blue sea

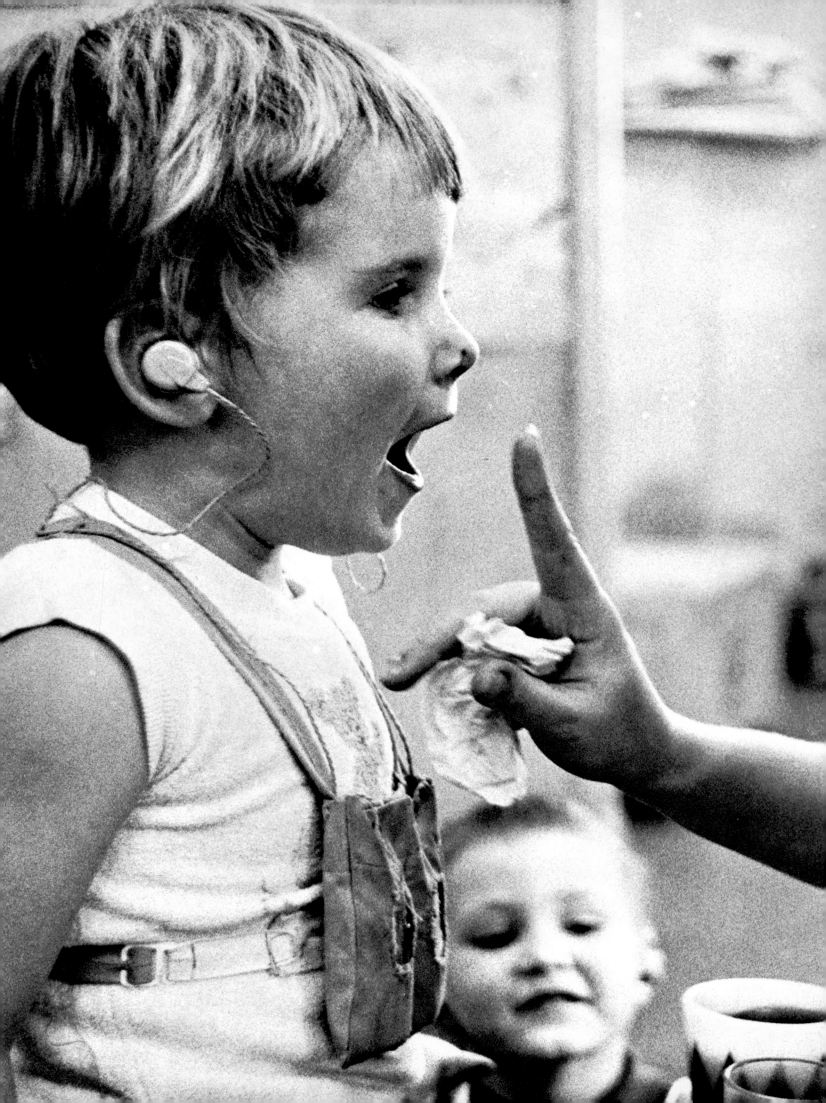

When a shell forsaken
by its creature lies,
the good of shellness
goes instead it holds
its shape as memorized;
frail and bleached
it curls like breath
(or death)
against the arm of the beach.

Or else brought here it lies
dry and intricate
upon my desk
(remembering the sea)
or winking with irony
at my child and me?

The distant bridge
hums iron lullabies,
the machines dream
they are ballet dancers
and fold like swans
into their metal wings;
          typewriters freeze
to enamelled silence;
in shipping rooms a man
looks up   somewhere
an old woman crosses herself
and two girls whisper together
and laugh.
          Everywhere
the people are spread out
like white beehives in green fields;
they are sunning themselves
like the explorers
          of a new time.

From the garish palazzo and
the city's heaving sea of light
the lamps shine with bravura and
the lonely love of middle age;

the many-layered ships
of the high rise buildings
sway in the wind   are sharp
and thin as knife cuts

in the landscape of time are
sharp as the graze of thorns
on my third eye which
remembers that somewhere

under its transparencies
floats my second eye   and
under it my first eye   the
earliest of all   it sees

somewhere in a neglected
field the beards of milkweed
and the shells of dry old men
and remembers that the wind

riffles somewhere through your
grey hair with fading laurel
leaves   and I see with all my
three eyes how your eyes

are dark as almond hearts
and smooth as the inside
of almond shells   how they
are filled with the years

bitter and stormy that
you buried somewhere
deep in the earth   how your
eyes have travelled far

beyond the light starry
touch of any young ghost
and how under the lamp
your eyes shine with bravura

the lonely love of middle age

Gentle becomes her;
like the white frill
falling over the wrist
rounds her with grace.

And the Queen Anne's lace
her whiteness insists
when she moves or is still
gentle must love her.

Tender as dove silk
her sleeves shake out clover
and sweet as the bee milk
night stirs in its cover.

Yet no light disturbs
her billowing bright
and no cloud perturbs
her gentle her white.

144

Let darkness stay and in the mirror deepen
ward daylight off lest sun
like a cruel painter seize
the honest stuff of morning to erase
us shadowy   illusory   and other.

Thin seabird you bend
to break the welling
waters   you drink
the pilgrim waters
divine the holy springs;
tread on speckled shells
and walk on bleached
and lemony wood,
you bend whitecollared
grey over the pink
stones and stand in sand
on one slender leg
listening.

And the pier-post sunbleached sings:
(eow eow it sings
soon it will be high tide
to drown all empty things
the sea wells up its springs)

Over the black
fountain   keyed   locked
in lifting music
you bend
lightwebbed frail;
across the whitening
beach breaks the sea
and from the sand
there wells
a fanning motion
the lapping waters
rise.

And the pier-post sunbleached sings:
(eow eow it sings
soon it will be high tide
to drown all empty things
the sea wells up its springs)

Thin seabird greyspun
tern   bending bird
beside the sea   thin
as a cardboard cutout
you sway
the moving wind
bent pilgrim listen
listen
to the welling waters
divine the holy springs.

And the pier-post sunbleached sings:
(eow eow it sings
soon it will be high tide
to drown all empty things
the sea wells up its springs)

from 'The Glass Trumpet'
OXFORD UNIVERSITY PRESS, Toronto, 1966

I wait the turned key   the sign;
our mother life does bless
me full of promises,
she holds out this goodnight
this small caress:
"It is not time, my child, sleep;
in time it will be time
and time enough and
such a time will keep,
such a time will keep."

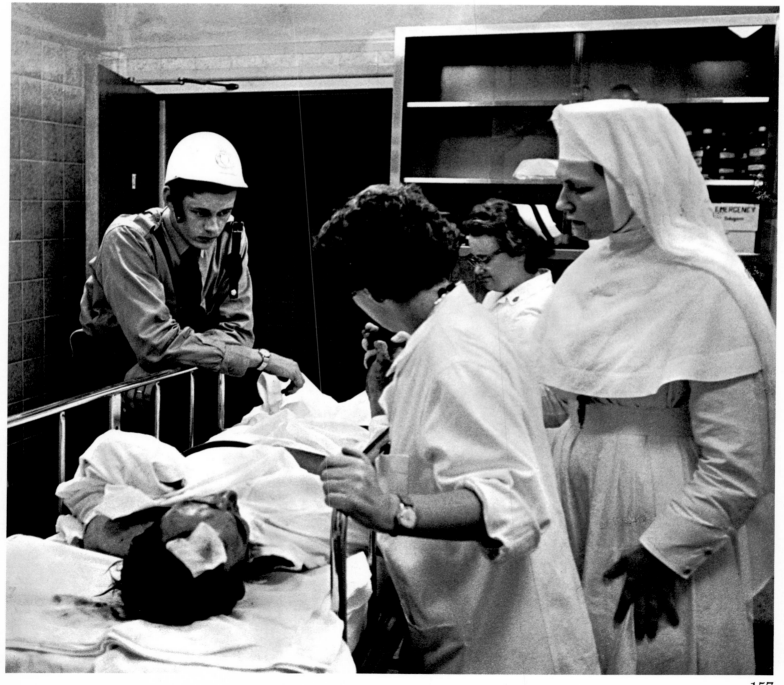

Death pursues us all; with gentle teeth
he nibbles at our edges and his loving tongue
seeks out key veins to mark them with a bruise;
fatuous, possessed, we wait for news
of his accomplishment and daily read
the local write-ups of his changing views

In the big city
wind assaulted her
dark voices shuttered her
chaos threatened her.

A forest of faces grew
thick on the edge of night
hot smiles crowded her
loose elbows jostled her.

Among faces anonymous
was one she recognized
the hunter loneliness
had stalked and followed her.

She turns now and runs
to buildings to shelter her
her feet hold to earth
the mother who nourished her.

Relentless the hunter
through the night follows her
hate his ragged hound
knows love is her camouflage

Furious they stalk the night
through the jungle streets,
terror spills its stars
over her leopard flight

And fear now feels its shape
alter with every hour
until child of itself in her
fear is reborn

New and apart from her:
at dawn they separate
childless in empty streets
hunter covers his sightless eyes.

163

Will there come a time
when flinging wide
the windows and the doors
butterflies will come
and gay restore
a nourishing future
to the mangy leaf?

Who mothered the eggs
that on the craggy grass
hang without signature?
Orphaned in the field
they lie and wait for sun
to come and breed
them warm to nature
and true to all their past.

Old woman cabbage queen
gourd-tapper fortune —
hunter in teacups
the black plumes
of your hatboat
quiver in the wind
tremble with secret
piracy as your knowing
hand touches without
gloves the supreme
trophy of the world's
cargo — peppersquash.

When you come home
to your rooming house
with the reddest apple
the most grooved most
crenellated peppersquash
the other old ladies
will vote you the
prize for picking you
will be snow-white and
rose-red you will be
royal at last
queening it in the
communal kitchen of
your rooming house

One two button my shoe;
(no one tells me what to do).

Three four shut the door;
(will I won't I win some more)?

Five six pick up sticks;
(this is how I get my kicks).

Seven eight lay them straight;
(it's certainly legitimate).

Nine ten a nice fat hen;
(only if I win again).

faces have no words
drums have no song
those who strain their ears
hear human voices soar
to a new pitch outside
their volume embraces piano
contains all violins
and floods the piccolos
such listeners can hear
old alarms turn off and
the new sound track spin

In the house of maimed desire
he will take your dreams of fire
and melt them into lead;
he will give you dancing girls
and color nightmares red or
style a snake on your back
so the coiled cylinder moves:
his needle dances with light,
his eyes are heavy and black.

His eyes are smithies of night
forging dreams of fire
in the city's burning groves,
and his house of maimed desire
is the graveyard of your loves.

No Lampman writes you poems now
no Varley strides to paint anew
the northern lakes of paradise
the lightning anger of our skies.

No sound will stir the prairie night
no Riel cry revolt through you
Mackenzie's words will compensate
for everything that's less than great;

Tom Thomson's savage brush once drew
the west wind braver than he knew,
but who to wilderness of slum
will now with sweeping colors come?

Your gods are written out in ink
on billboards panoramic screens,
they bless the decade praise this day
and pioneer the middle way.

Love
remember me
as I do you   our
locked voices and
morning mists over
the city   how
we hung in the
transparent bell
of summer and
swayed to the
rhythm of an
accordion-folded
sun

Of all my broken
selves of all my
patterns are you
everywhere on every
page on every hour
in every color is
your design in
leaf shapes and
flower shapes in
every color of
time in every
shape of time

It is all writ-
ten in the leaves
in the flowers of
the kaleidoscope
and why are
the trees bare
where do the old
rained-out choirs
sing in what world
and does autumn
flood the town and
are the rivers
marlowe colored?

In N town and no
town in my wintry
lover's ghost town
in the snowmists
of paperweights
on the bleak plat-
forms of railway
stations on the
mountain peaks
of winnipeg in the
sealed up cottages
of summer in the
locked wells the

shadows in win-
dows in the flow-
ers of kaleido-
scopes in the illu-
sion of returning
in the shape of
the leaves in the
dark of your face
in the gravel of
your voice in the
summer of your words

In the winter
under your words
where the light
of sunflowers
is locked away
where I love
the time I
looked in you
and loved the
purity I found
in you and lost
the question
I gave to you

And the autumn
is immediate the
sun strikes and
how helpless
I am against
the purity in you
against the dis-
solving patterns
and how dazzling
how dazzling are
these leaves the
miraculous dark
marlowe flowers

he will bury
the sharp rocks of longing
seven fathoms below
consciousness
and she
will spread herself
a sighing caress
in the seagreen
                    sunlight
filtered
through oceans of sorrow

lovers tread the waters
lovers go
in all the seasons
where the waters flow
they neither swim nor fly
but float in trees
and magically they go
where all the world envies
where they go.

from 'Second Silence'
RYERSON PRESS, Toronto, 1955

In this see-saw between skin and soul
the artist takes the part of balancer,
his touch is fatal yet it must be sure,
his purpose total since he has to race
the death which lurks disguised in every face;

And what if painting life he finds
that he has drawn age, disquietude?
his chalk enshrines:
and now his love must keep
death soft in draperies
with wonderful green feet.

We see in dead of dark
and find the face of night
we touch the side of day
and grasp the edge of light

It's raining in Toronto   love
I wonder what it's doing
in Fredericton   he didn't
come home last night
did he   men are like birds
cat-escapers   rain drives
them away   smoke drives them
away   a woman has to know
that every dog has his day
and when he's gone
he's gone   so

cheer up   love
come under my umbrella
there's room for three

They live in their country,
we live in ours,
we share a road, a lake, the sun,
all the attributes of place.

We walk in twos,
they go in fours,
for we are few and they
with all the bravery of birth

Take pride in numbers;
and this reads
innocently in each fair
and blue-eyed face.

We are outside and they are in;
uneasily we breathe the air
which they so cleverly divide,
and wear as casual as a cape
which them reveals, but us must hide.

Lonely as indefinite sin
we take the air, go for a stroll;
we share the attributes of place,
but we are broken, they are whole.

The lilies are lying prone
stems broken and long alone,
say no more.

However much we sigh
the graves will multiply,
say no more.

In the cold salt mines of the sea
the dragon wears a crown and
the fish break like rainbows
in clouds of water

Beyond the white gothic of her smile
far pools of stillness lie
and the summer wind
plays the green mandolins of her voice,
her words are plain as ballads and they sing
the flowering season and the moving space
between waking and sleeping
and then the final sleep

from 'Second Silence'
RYERSON PRESS, Toronto, 1955

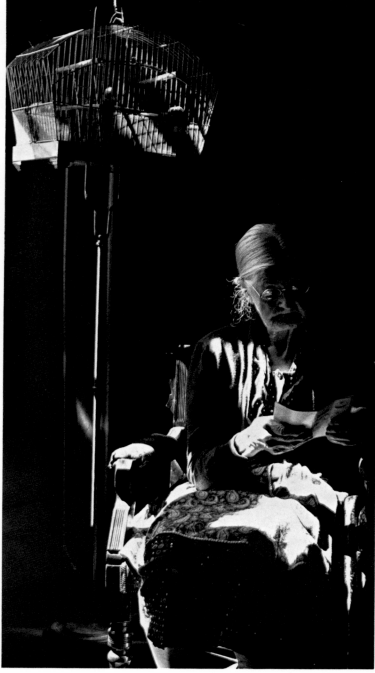

I look up through boughs of snow
at faces of poets I know and don't know
they float around me motherless Poe
preacher Donne who bewitched a crowd
and William Blake who sang aloud
the paradigm of humankind.

Their faces waver their voices throw
dark-printed words against the snow
with the shudder of love or clammy touch
of a small sick animal: what do I know?
The sky through the boughs is blue as a flag
and grows more distant every minute.

Bluer than blue is the sky and cold;
this must be what the poets told
of a clearer vision in smaller space
in the land of their never growing old;
the random scattering of snow and
time will cover all they know but

the contours of their sleeping thought
will awaken into life again when
maps, those late at night diversions,
unfold and are followed by the curious;
a mountain once closed on a cloud of
children a frog spouted pearls a girl's

hair was the ladder that spanned
our divided worlds their words are fires
their faces promises in the snow and
the blind eye of father Milton shines
beyond his daughter's night of sorrow,
his brow is a beacon of steady light

and his arm coated with hoary frost
has cleared us a road archangel white.

Little father your
rhythmic black robe
against white snow
improvises you
a black note
on a white keyboard;

let me follow
into your churchbarn
through the gate
to the onion domes
where your carrot
harvest burns
a fire of candles,

let me follow
in the cool light
as you move through
God's storehouse
as you put the bins
in order as you set
each grain in place;

let me follow
as your voice
moves in the
familiar liturgy
through the low caves
of gregorian chant
and let me hear
little father

how you pray
for all your geese
for the cow fertile
at easter and the
foundations of new
houses to be strong
and firmly set;

let me hear
how you beseech
for all your people
a clear road   an
open gate and
a new snowfall
fresh   dazzling
white as birchbark.

Prophet dream us a palm of light
and make it bloom in our hands
until Friday's festival
spreads its peace like wings
over the unquiet world.
Fold us smooth as shining hair
of a pious wife in slumbers sweet
then wake us fresh with Sabbath bread
from enchanted sleep and look
with us past the templed ruins:
deep as the cratered earth
plumb our purpose and hallowed be
the heady wine of our hope.

208

Will we defeat the death
that waits within these walls
(and in the world outside)?
And will we from the rain
the soot the hundred-year-old stains
from tired travelling,
find sleep unhaunted and
get the strength to build
palaces whose walls
stay white against the rain,
marbled and mild?

from 'The Second Silence'
RYERSON PRESS, Toronto, 1955

The happiness of birds
and pianos sounding
the shining dish of stones
where turtles turn
and fish that silent streak
the white aquarium,
the happiness of children
busy with cries and games
and underneath the stairs
the cricket singing.

How does the seed grow
in what city is the wheel
that turns the world
Montreal or Winnipeg?
We do not know.

The best we know
is like the child asleep
helpless   a face
with sorrows deep   the best
we have is that we're partly
old and partly young   but

Best there is
and this best we give;
to nature's question
our answer is:
turn the world and shelter us
the wheel is in the seed.

Time is the teacher
and summer the favored child
who takes instruction
as it's really meant;
and what a pleasure
in bright rooms and mild
to move content
with nature's government,
and for each ritual moment
of the day
to dress in celebration
and to bring
each winter's end
to unexpected spring

The sun-stroked birds
the tipped-with-yellow-
crowned-with-royal-red
feathers that blaze
the still pine woods;
the dunes hush-studded
transitory earth-grappling
grinning in the spread
of gnarled roots
that riffle up their sides,
the purpling plum the
climbing ocean wave   all
for a moment stop   hang
brilliant and amazed.

There is a man who calls me wife
who knows me but does not know my life
and my two sons who call me mother
see me not as any other
yet if the fabric of my day
should be unwound and fall away
what colored skeins would carelessly
unwind where I live secretly?

Penelope among the dandelions stood:
wild trees her suitors were,
the passionate winds made of the years a blur
and time went hungry except when seasons
nourished and gave food.

Penelope to the park on Sundays came:
she fed the ducks and through a wire net
pushed popcorn to a camel who lives yet;
she led a tottering child on a leash
and called him by his name,

Tom or Telemachus, and what was her mood
in Corfu or Toronto as she scanned the field
hedged by buildings and by waters heeled?
She dreamed an ocean shimmered at her feet
and mourned a Grecian wood.

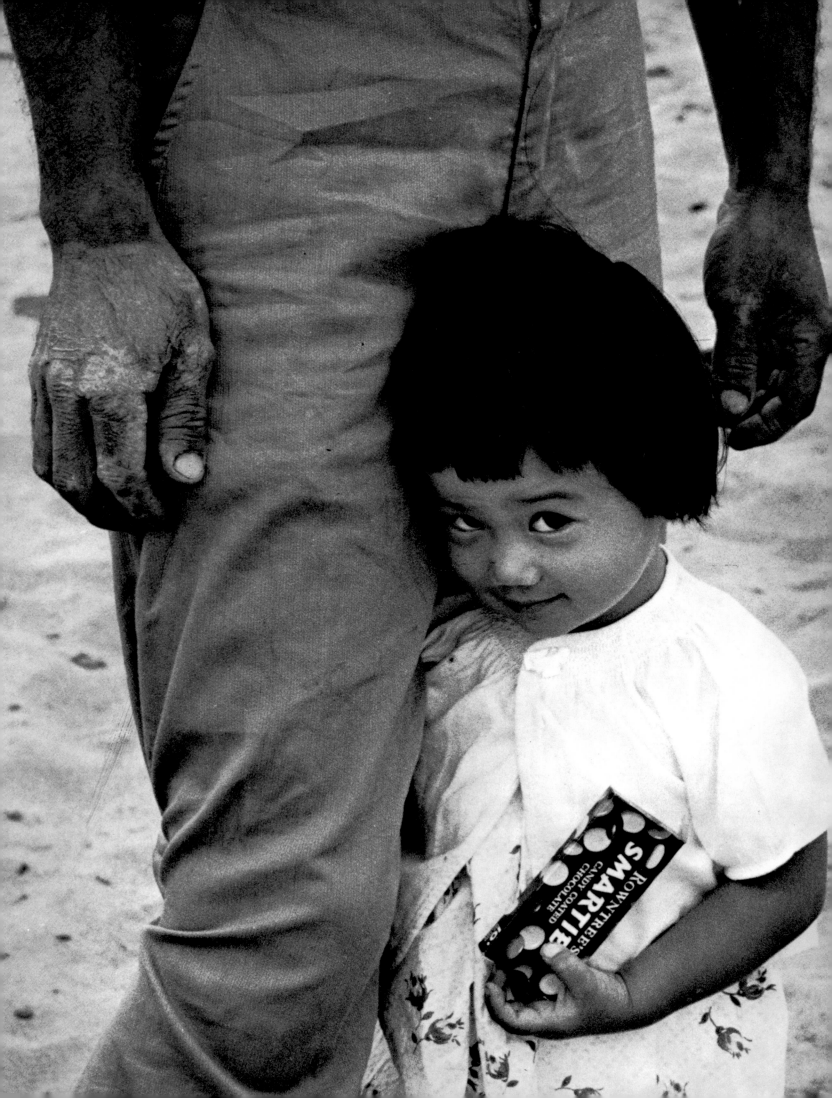

I am not Pacific
I am not Atlantic
I have no Arabian movement
nor Byzantian flavor,
I own a dry square of prairie
in a middle province   bordered
by a mile of wire fence   squeezed
between mountain ranges
deprived of a forest and
starved for an ocean.

I have a criss-cross
of muddy roads   a geometry
of railway tracks a couple
of clapboard shacks and
a scant scrubble of bush;
nothing but humdrum
the whole year round
I can still boast of
one royal moment when
the full warm wheat
of August grows tall
and green as our children.

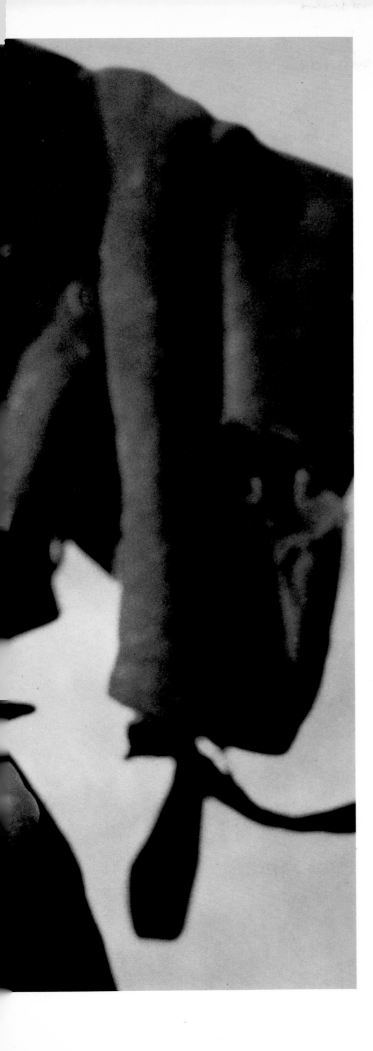

What is this love of country and of street?
It is fable it is foreign curved gables
across a river   suns that mourn the liquid
sounds of every alien tongue.

It is clutch and clamp at pit of stomach
shudder in the small of back at sight
of opening autumn which achingly transmutes
through all its portals this one fixed view:

The distant city formed by the thrust
Of blackened chimney   flaming sky
And milk-looped roofless clouds
And all   all the yearning crowd of

Moving people   the laced conglomerate
of leaves and ferns   the timeless measure
of each mortal moment and the dance.

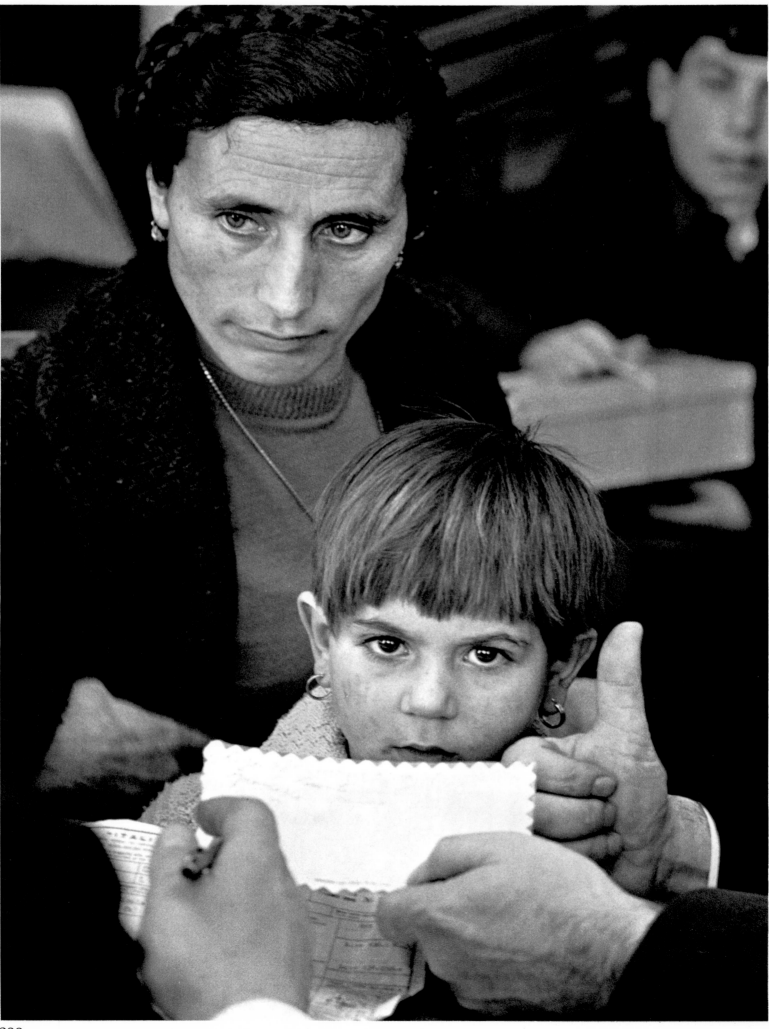

We are caught in a dry net
knotted and well-tied;
each in his separate loop
we wash against the tide,
to glancing passers-by
we seem alike
but when identified
each one becomes himself
and fits a different shell.

Here are
our signatures:
geese fish eskimo
faces girl-guide
cookies ink-drawings
tree-plantings summer
storms and winter
emanations.

We look
like a geography
but just scratch us
and we bleed like
history are full
of modest misery
sensitive
to double-talk double-take
(and double-cross)
in a country
too wide
to be single in.

Are we real or
did someone invent
us was it Henry
Hudson Etienne Brulé
or a carnival
of village girls?
Was it a flock of nuns
a pity of Indians
a gravyboat of
fur-traders professional
explorers or those
amateur map-makers
our Fathers
of Confederation?

Wherever you are
Charles Tupper Alexander
Galt D'Arcy McGee George
Cartier Ambrose Shea
Henry Crout Father
Ragueneau Lord Selkirk
and John A: however
far into northness
you have walked
when we call you turn
around please and
don't look so
surprised.

INDEX